More than
650 Pictures -
All in COLOUR

Rapidex®
CHILDREN'S Dictionary

Animated audio visual DVD helping your child learn correct pronunciation

Rapidex®

CHILDREN'S Dictionary

More than 650 Pictures - All in COLOUR

Published by

Rapidex PUBLICATIONS

An imprint of

PUSTAK MAHAL®

Administrative office and sale centre
J-3/16 , Daryaganj, New Delhi-110002
☎ 23276539, 23272783, 23272784 • *Fax:* 011-23260518
E-mail: info@pustakmahal.com • *Website:* www.pustakmahal.com

Branches
Bengaluru: ☎ 080-22234025 • *Telefax:* 080-22240209
E-mail: pustak@airtelmail.in • pustak@sancharnet.in
Mumbai: ☎ 022-22010941, 022-22053387
E-mail: rapidex@bom5.vsnl.net.in
Patna: ☎ 0612-3294193 • *Telefax:* 0612-2302719
E-mail: rapidexptn@rediffmail.com

ISBN 978-81-223-0278-3

Edition : 2014

Printed at : Tarun Printers, Delhi

a A

above: on top means **above**

The bird flies **above** the cat.

The cat jumps **above** the dog.

add: means when you measure

Addition is when you **add** up

You **add** 2 + 3 and get 5.

against

Against means to rest or lean.

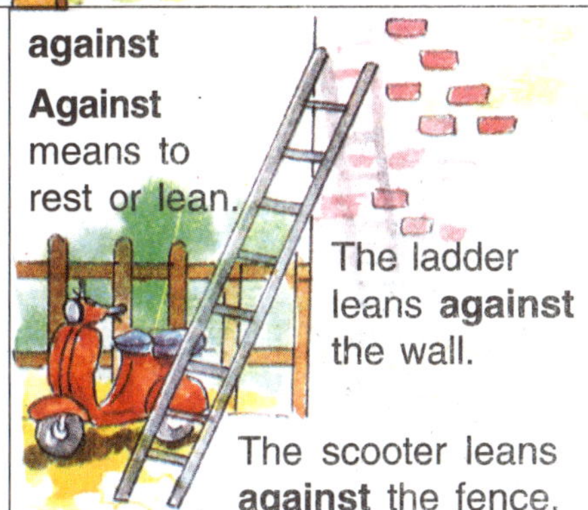

The ladder leans **against** the wall.

The scooter leans **against** the fence.

accident

Arun breaks a flask by mistake.

It is an **accident**.

address

An **address** is the detail of the place where you live

The **address** is written on a letter.

air

We breathe **air**; we cannot see it.

Balloons are filled with **air**.

acorn

Acorn is the fruit of the oak tree.

aeroplane

An **aeroplane** flies people to different places.

across: to go from one side to another

The children walk **across** the street.

An airport is where **aeroplanes** land and take off.

alike: when two things are the same

The twins are **alike**,
their dogs are not **alike**.

all

All means everything
All the flowers are red.

alone

Anita is on her own.

She is **alone**.

along: is to move from one end to the other end.

Arun and the cat walk **along** the wall.

alphabet: words are made of letters

Our **alphabet** has 26 letters.

always

Every time means **always**

Snow is **always** white
Coal is **always** black.

and

And is a joining word

Cup **and** saucer, fork **and** knife, bacon **and** egg.

angry

Being cross is **angry**

Asha is **angry**.

animal

Our **animal** world consists of birds, fishes and four-legged creatures.

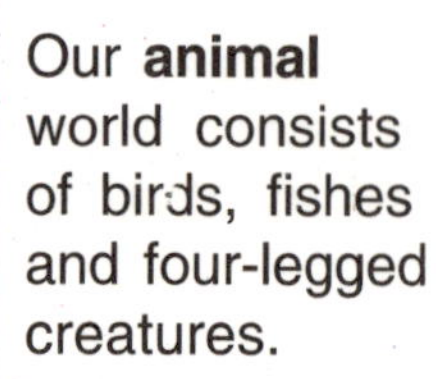

ankle

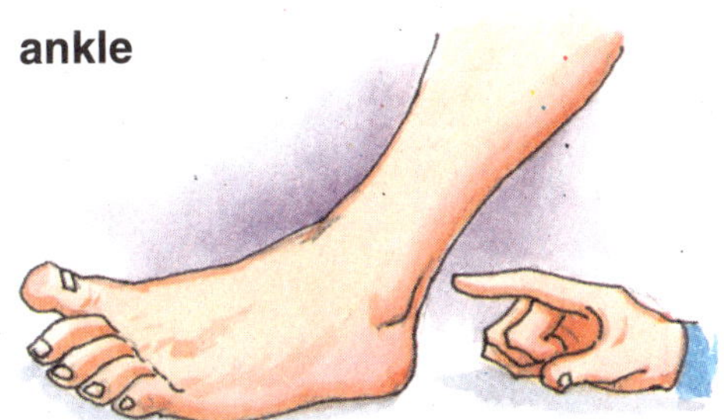

The joint between the foot and the leg

answer: when you reply to a question

You **answer** the telephone when it rings.

arm

We have two **arms**.

A chair also has **arms**.

arrow

An **arrow** is shot from a bow.

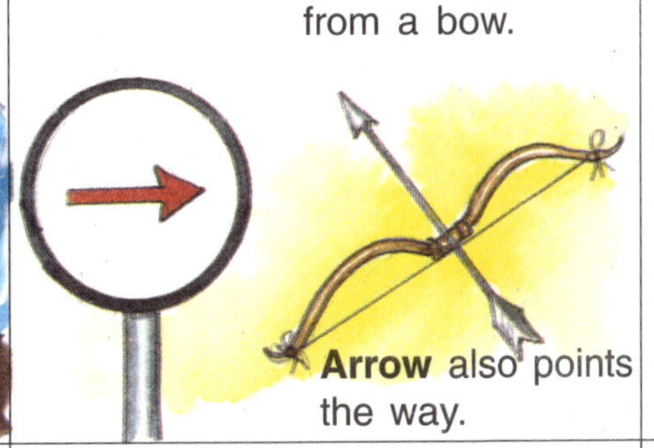

Arrow also points the way.

artist An **artist** draws and paints pictures

ask: You **ask** questions.

Arun **asks** his father the time.

asleep: not awake

The baby is **asleep**.

astronaut

An **astronaut** travels through space in a spaceship.

aunt

A female relative

Aunts are sisters of your mummy and daddy.

ant

An **ant** is a tiny insect that bites.

apple An **apple** is a sweet juicy fruit.

Apples are mostly red.

autumn: the season before winter

awake: not asleep

The baby is **awake**.

b B

baby: a very small child

The **baby** plays with a ball.

bake: to cook in the oven

Mummy has **baked** a cake.

bank: a place where money is kept

Men and women work in a **bank**.

back: not in the front.

Bobby and Bela are standing **back** to **back**.

ball and bat: things to play with

We hit the **ball** with the **bat**.

To return is to take it **back**.

Bela takes the book **back** to the library.

balloon

We blow air into **balloons**.

Balloons burst easily.

beach: land along the sea

A **beach** has sand.

bad: not good

This apple is **bad**.

This dog is **bad** too.

band: a group which plays music together

beak: the mouth of a bird

Birds eat with their **beaks**.

bed Bina sleeps on her **bed**.

Her dog has its own **bed**.

bee: an insect that makes honey

Have you seen a **beehive**?

bell

You ring a **bell**.
A church has a big **bell**.

belt: worn around the waist

Both the boys are wearing black **belts**.

between: in the middle of omething

A man is sitting **between** his children.

bicycle

A bicycle has two pedals.
Can you ride a **bicycle**?

big: when it is not small

The red truck is **big**.

The blue truck is **bigger**.

The yellow truck is the **biggest**.

bird

A **bird** has feathers and wings. Most **birds** can fly with their wings.

Or
Can you name these **birds**?

birthday: the day you were born

Bobby celebrates his fifth **birthday**.

biscuit

Biscuits are made with flour

Biscuits are crisp and mostly sweet to eat.

bite

We use our teeth to **bite**.

Bobby **bites** into an apple.

black: a dark colour

Black is the colour of coal.
This cat is **black**.

blackboard: the board on which teachers write

Every classroom has a **blackboard**.

blanket: a warm cover

The girl sleeps under a **blanket**.

blow

The wind **blows**.
Binoo **blows** a horn.

blue: a colour
A **blue** kite flies in the **blue** sky.

boat: a small hollow structure that sails on water

Boats come in different sizes.

book: a **book** contains pages with words and pictures

Have you read a story **book**?

both: two together

Both Bina and Tina have umbrellas.
Both the umbrellas are spotted.

bottom: something below

Bimal is at the **bottom** of the hill.

box: a box holds things

This **box** has cereals.

This **box** has chocolates.

bread
A baker bakes all kinds of **bread**.

We eat slices of **bread** with butter.

breakfast: the first meal of the day

Bela is eating her **breakfast**.

bubble

Bina is blowing **bubbles**. **Bubbles** burst easily.

busy: to be doing something

Mrs Behl is **busy** with housework.

brick

Bricks are used to build houses.

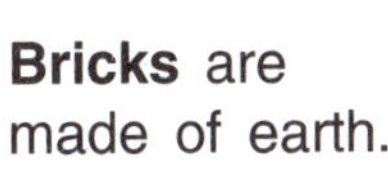

Bricks are made of earth.

build: to make something

butter: a smooth spread made from milk

Do you like your bread with **butter**?

bridge: connects two points of a river or road

A school, house, skyscraper are all **buildings**.

butterfly

A catterpillar turns into a **butterfly**.

Butterflies fly with their beautiful wings.

brown: a colour

This cow is **brown**.

This log is **brown** too.

button: holds clothes together

Can you **button** your shirt?

brush: something to tidy our hair with.

We **brush** our hair.
We **brush** our teeth with a **toothbrush**.

bus

A **bus** carries people to places.
Have you been on a **bus**?

buy: to pay money for something.

Bobby **buys** a boat.

c C

cage: where an animal or bird is kept

The parrot is in a **cage**.

can: a doing word
I **can** ride a bike.
A **can** holds things too.

A **can** of juice.

carpet

carpet: a cover for the floor

cake

Cakes are made with flour and raisins

Rina is making a **cake**.

candle: made of wax, gives light when lit

Nisha is putting **candles** on a cake.

carry: to take a thing from one place to another

Rahul is **carrying** his books and a bag.

calendar: a chart showing dates, months in a year

Ramesh is looking at the **calendar**.

car

A **car** has four wheels
You drive a **car**.

castle
Kings and queens live in a **castle**.

You can make **castles** out of sand.

camera

Camera takes pictures of people and places

Sonia is taking a photograph with the **camera**.

careful: to be cautious

Be **careful** when you cross the street.

cat: a furry animal.

Cats chase rats.

Farmers chase **cats**.

caterpillar: a worm found on trees

Caterpillars turn into a butterfly.

chair: something to sit on

A **chair** has legs and arms too.

cheese

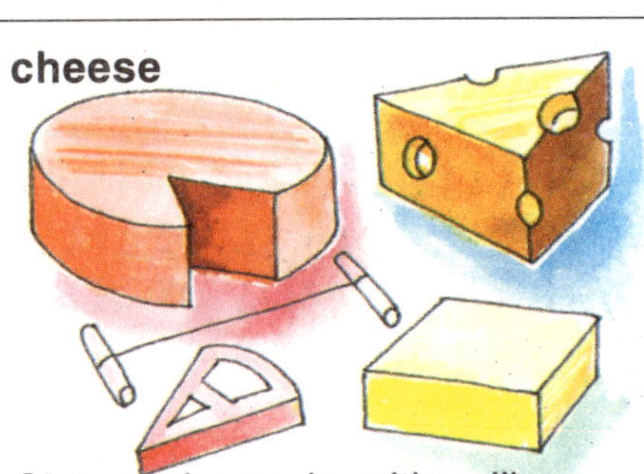

Cheese is made with milk.
Cheese is soft and good to eat.

chest: a body's upper front part.

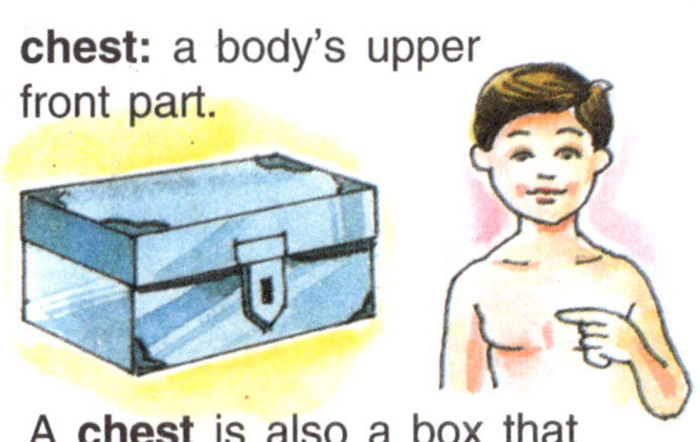

A **chest** is also a box that holds things.

child: a young person

Are you a **child**?

Christmas: the birthday of Jesus.

Christmas is celebrated on December 25 every year.

church: a place where Christians worship.

Have you seen a **church**?

circle: a round shape.

The sun is a **circle**.

circus: a show with clowns and animals

Have you been to a **circus**?

animals

clowns

acrobats

city: a very big town

Men and women work in a **city**.

classroom: a room in a school

Students learn from a teacher in a **classroom**.

cloud

Clouds float in the sky.

Clouds are white or gray.

clean: without dirt

Rahul's face is **clean**.

Bobby's face is not **clean**.

climb: to go up

The child is **climbing** the stairs.

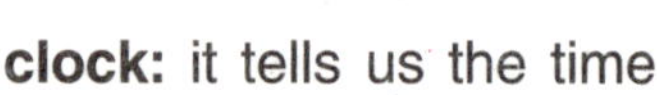

clock: it tells us the time

Clocks come in many sizes.

clothes: we wear these on our body

jacket

pyjamas

dress

coat

shirt

gloves

skirt

scarf

trousers

jumper

t-shirt, jumper are **clothes**.

clown: a joker

Clowns are found in a circus.

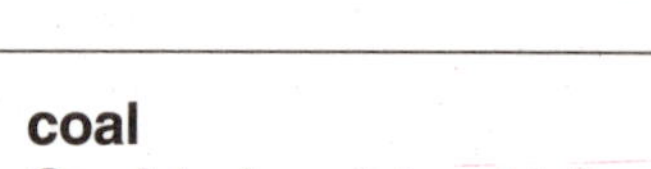

coal

Coal is burnt to get fire

Coal is hard and black.

coat: a jacket to keep us warm

Sheep have **coats** too.

cobweb

A **cobweb** is a fine net a spider spins around itself.

coffee: a hot drink

Coffee is made with cocoa beans.

cold: not hot

Snow is **cold**.

You sneeze when you catch **cold**.

colour: everything has a colour

The **colour** of the flowers is yellow.

The **colour** of the ball is red.

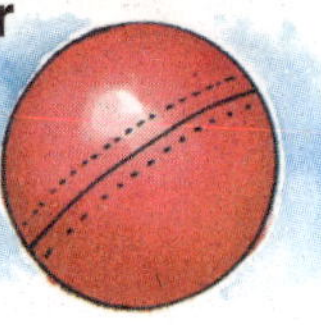

comb: used to tidy our hair

Combs have teeth.

cook
Mummy **cooks** lunch

A male **cook** is called a chef.

count: to add up figures or money

The man **counts** the numbers.

cover: to put something on

The baby has a **cover** on him.

crawl: to walk on all fours
Insects **crawl** too.

cry You **cry** when you are hurt or in pain.

When you **cry**, you have tears in your eyes.

cup
We drink milk from a **cup**.

A **cup** is a prize too.

curtain: a covering for doors and widows

Curtains are mostly made with cloth.

cut: You use scissors or knife to **cut**.

You can **cut** and hurt yourself.

d D

dance: move to music

Dona is **dancing**.

danger: harmful

This is a **danger** sign.

dark: means without light

The night is **dark**.

date: what day, month or year it is

A **date** is a sweet fruit.

day: comes before night

There is sunlight during the **day**.

decide: to make up one's mind

Dina cannot **decide** which toy to play with.

Saurabh cannot **decide** which sweets to eat.

deep: to go below the surface

Oceans are **deep**.

dentist: the doctor who cares for our teeth

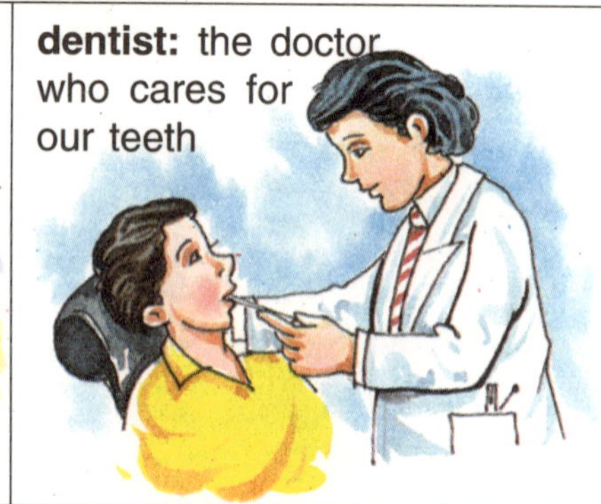

describe: to say something more

Can you **describe** this dress?

desert: a large sandy area

Camels live in a **desert**.

desk: a table where we study or draw

Anita is studying a book on her desk.

dictionary: a book with words and their meanings

This is a picture **dictionary**.

different: not the same
These ducks are **different**.

The cars are **different** too.

The picture shows **different** things.

dig:

Dilip is **digging** the soil with a spade.

You **dig** before you plant.

dive: to jump into the water

The boy **dives** into the pool.

divide: to **divide** means to split into parts, or to share.

Mummy **divides** the pie into three pieces.

Dog We keep **dogs** as pets.

Can you name these **dogs**?

boxer

bulldog

greyhound

spaniel

poodle

great dane

dachshund

sheepdog

husky

difficult: not easy

Dilip finds his lesson **difficult**.

Doctor: a person who treats the sick

We wait at the **doctor's** chamber.

doll: a toy

The **doll** sits inside a **doll**'s house.

donkey: a small horse-like animal

door Houses have **doors** to let people in.

Dilip opens the **door**.

down: not up

Dina is walking **down** the street.

downstairs: the lower part of a house

Rahul is going **downstairs**.

draw: to make a picture

Do you like to **draw**?

drawer: a place to keep things in

There are 3 **drawers** in this chest.

dream: when we see pictures in our mind

We **dream** when we sleep.

drink: a liquid

Can I take this cold **drink**, mummy?

drive: when you make something move

The man is **driving** a bus.

The woman is **driving** a car.

drop

Rain**drops** are falling.

Dilip **drops** a ball.

drum: a musical instrument

We beat a **drum** with sticks.

dry: not wet

The wind **dries** our clothes.

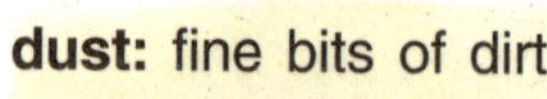

The lady makes her hand **dry**.

dust: fine bits of dirt

Rahul is removing the **dust** from the furniture.

e E

ear
We hear with our **ears**.

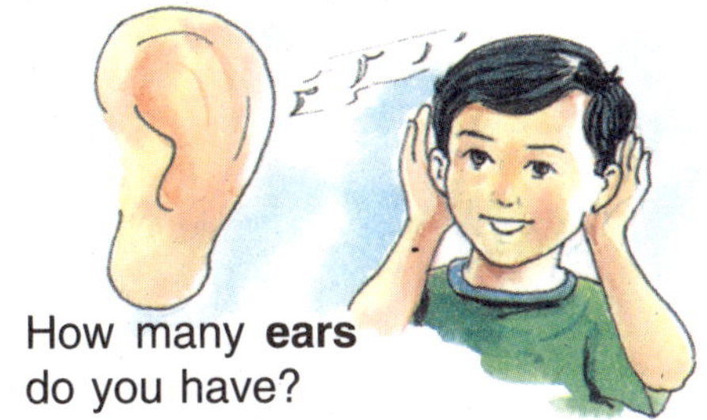

How many **ears** do you have?

easy: not hard.

Tina draws pictures **easily.**

egg A hen lays an **egg**.

Chicks are born from hen's **eggs**.

early: to be before time.

The school bus has come **early** today.

eat: when you bite, chew & swallow food

Anil is **eating** a burger.

eight: is a number.

There are **eight** balls on the table.

earth

We live on planet **Earth**.

The soil is also the **earth**.

echo: a sound that bounces back

An **echo** is heard in caves and mountains.

elbow

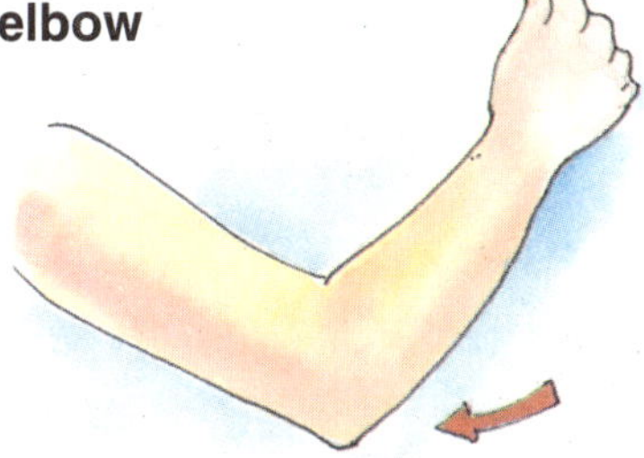

An **elbow** joins the arm with the hand.

edge: on the brink.

A knife has an **edge**.

The vase is on the table's **edge**.

electricity

Electricity makes lights and fans work.
Machines run on **electricity**.

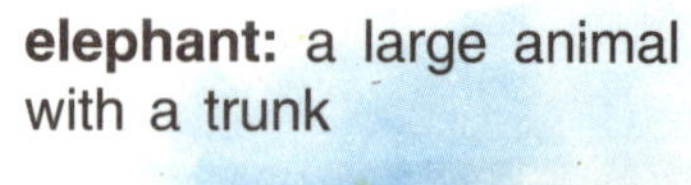

elephant: a large animal with a trunk

This is a huge **elephant**.

eleven: a number between ten and twelve

There are **eleven** elephants.

empty: means nothing.

Isha's purse is **empty**.

end: to finish something

The boys are holding on to the rope's **ends**.

engine: makes a machine work

Trains have **engines**.
A car has an **engine** too.

enormous: is very big

Harsh holds an **enormous** ice cream.

enough: just the right amount.

Ena has **enough** money for this toy.

envelope

A letter or money is put inside an **envelope**.

escalator: is a moving stairway

Escalators are found in public places.

evening: part of the day that comes before night.

every: means all

Every morning we wake up

We eat breakfast **every** morning.

exit: means way out

Have you seen the **exit** sign?

eye
We see with our **eyes**.

Ajay has a pair of black **eyes**.

f F

face: the front part of the head

A **face** has eyes, nose, mouth.

fall: to drop down

The apple **falls** from the tree.

fasten: to join two things

Mummy **fastens** the car seat belt.

fact: not a lie

This is a dog – it's a **fact**.

family: people you live with at home

A **family** consists of mummy, daddy, brothers and sisters.

fat: not thin

Ravi is **fatter** than Ritu.

factory: a place where things are made

Factories give out thick smoke.

farm: where crops are grown Animals live in a **farm**.

feel: you **feel** when you touch something

Feel the cat's furry coat – it's soft.

fail: when you do not succeed

The fox **fails** to reach for the grapes.

A **farmer** looks after a farm.

fence: a barrier that protects crops and animals

few: means less

Nisha has a **few** marbles.

fight: to quarrel

The boys are **fighting** over a ball.

fill: when you make it full

Rahul **fills** his glass with milk.

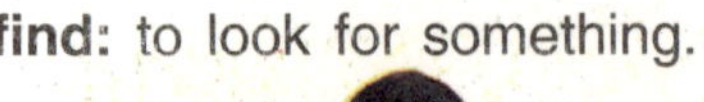

field: an open green space

Anil is playing in the **field**.

find: to look for something.

Fatima **finds** her doll under the table.

finger: your hand has 5 fingers

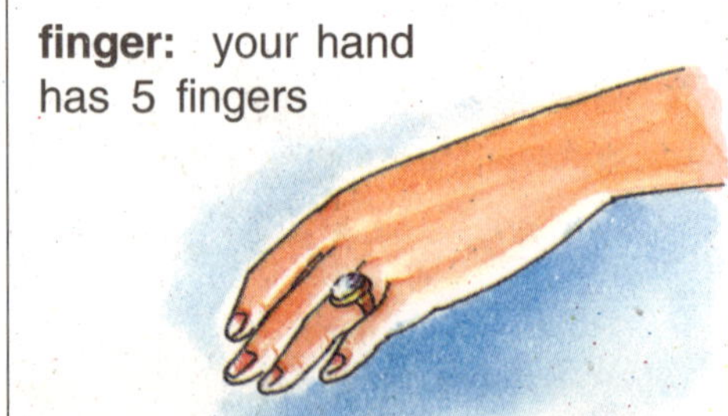

You can wear a ring on your **finger**.

finish: to complete a task.

Daddy **finishes** reading the story.

fire: when something is burnt

In case of a big **fire**, a **fire** engine is called.

first: before others

Ajay comes **first** in the race.

fish: an animal that lives in water

There are many kinds of **fish**.

fit: to be of the correct size

Rahul's mother sees if his shoes **fit**.

five: a number between four and six

There are **five** flowers in the picture.

flag: the symbol of every country

The Indian **flag** has 3 colours.

flat: a level area

A table top is **flat**.

Flats are many houses in a single building.

float: when something stays on water without sinking.

Boats and ships **float** on water.

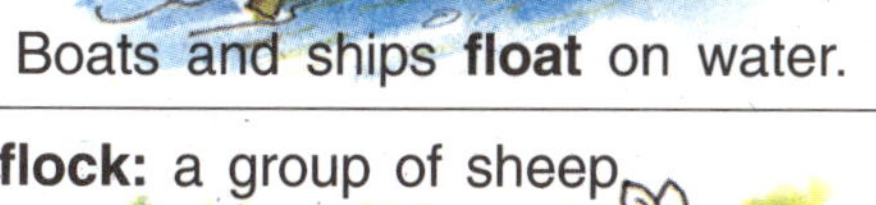

flock: a group of sheep

floor: the part of room we walk on

The baby is on the **floor**.

flower: part of a plant from which the seed or food develops.

Flowers are very pretty.

rose

daffodil

daisy

buttercup

iris

fly: a small insect with wings.

Birds and aeroplanes **fly** with their wings.

fog: a covering of thick mist

We find it difficult to see in a **fog**.

follow: to go after somebody

The dog is **following** Rashmi.

food: things we eat

Can you name these different kinds of **food**?

apple

foot: where the leg ends

We have two **feet**.
The dog has four **feet**.

forest: a forest is a thick jungle

Wild animals live in a **forest**.

forget: when you do not remember

Nitin's sister tells him not to **forget** his books.

four: a number between three and five.

There are **four** birds in the picture.

free: when it does not cost money.

An entry to the park is **free**.

freeze: when water becomes ice

The pond is **frozen**.

friend: somebody you are close to

Nisha and Anita are **friends**.

front
Agrim is standing in **front** of the tree

His name is on the **front** of his shirt.

fruit: it holds the tree's seed and can be eaten as food.

Can you name all these **fruits**?

funny: not sad

Clowns are **funny**.

fur: the soft hair on the animal's body

The polar bear has white **fur**.

furniture: things we use in our homes
Bed, chair, table are all **furniture**.

g G

game We play a **game** to relax.

hide and seek

Football and cricket are **games**.

football

cricket skipping rope

gift: a present

We receive **gifts** on our birthday.

giraffe: a very tall animal with a long neck

A **giraffe** has spots on its body.

garage: a place where a car is kept

A large **garage** repairs cars.

gate

a door through which you enter a house or garden.

glass: is hard and clear.

We see ourselves in the **glass**.

A **glass** holds liquid too.

garden: a small patch of land with grass and flowers

get: to obtain something

"How much money did you **get**?" Gita asks Girish.

glove

We wear **gloves** on our hands to keep them warm.

goat: an animal with horns

A **goat** gives us milk.

gold: a yellow metal

Gold is made into jewellery.

goldfish: a golden-coloured fish

Goldfishes are kept as a pet.

goodbye
You wave **goodbye** when someone goes away.

goose: a large duck

A **goose** has webbed feet.

gorilla: a very big monkey

Gorillas are found in Africa.

grandparents

Grandparents are parents of our mummy and daddy.

grape: small sweet fruit

Grapes grow in bunches.

grass: a small plant growing on the ground

Cows eat **grass**.

green: is a colour

Pea is **green**.

Leaves are **green**.

group: when there are a few people together

This is a **group** of children.

grow: when something becomes big from small

The sunflower is **growing** in size.

growl: an angry sound

The lion and dog are both **growling**.

guess: when we are not sure about something

Nisha is trying to **guess** what is in the box.

guitar: a musical instrument with strings

This is a very costly **guitar**.

h H

hair: what grows on your head.

Nisha has long black **hair**.

handle: something to hold with
Pans, mugs and doors have **handles**.

hat: something worn on the head

Hats come in many sizes.

half: when you divide something into two

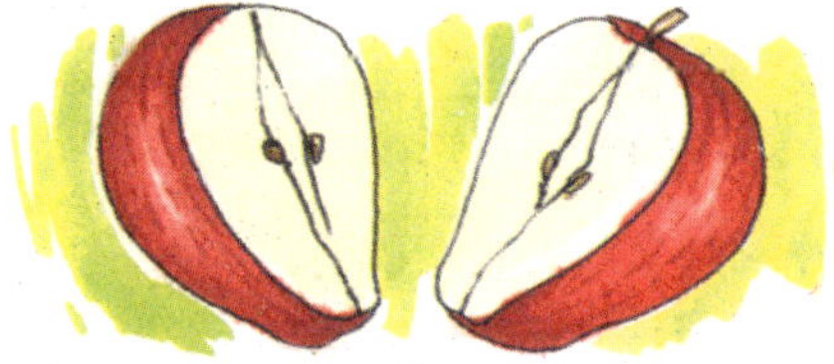

Two **halves** are alike.

happy: not sad

We smile when we are **happy**.

head: the upper part of our body

Hari is at the **head** of the line.

hand: to hold things and work with

The clock also has **hands**.

hard: not soft, solid, firm.

hear: organs we listen with
What does this girl **hear**? Music!

handkerchief: a piece of cloth to wipe our face

hard is not easy.
Hiren finds it **hard** to ride a bicycle.

heart

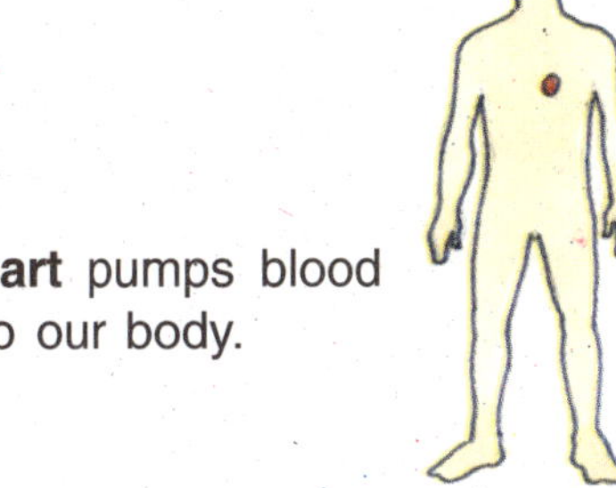

Heart pumps blood into our body.

heavy: something with a great weight

Raju cannot lift the **heavy** suitcase.

heel: the back part of a foot

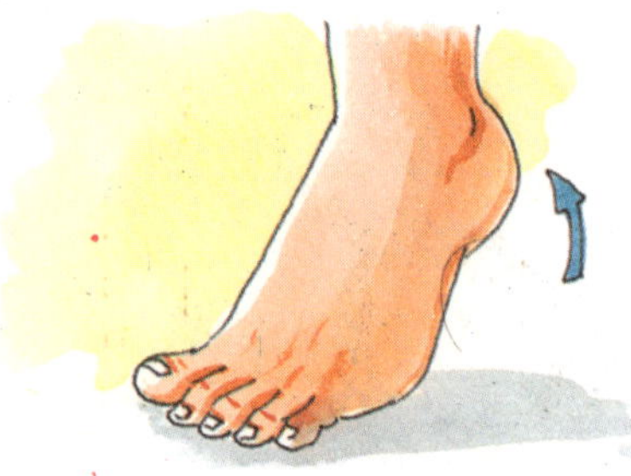

helicopter: a small aeroplane

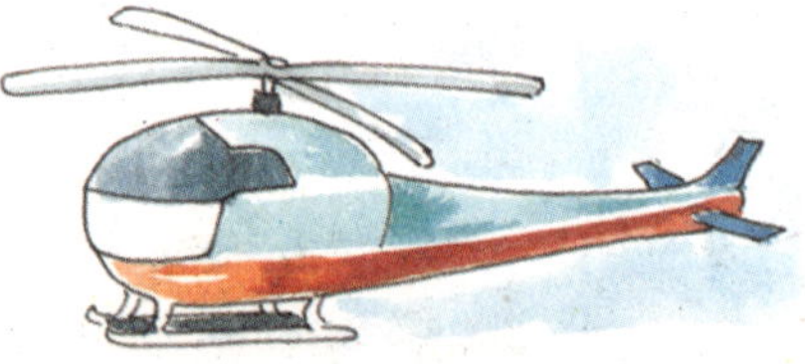

A **helicopter** has blades instead of wings.

hello: a means of greeting

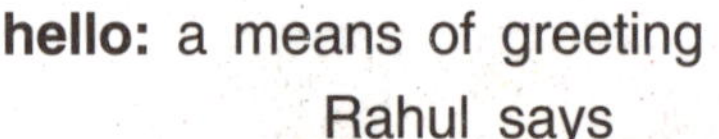

Rahul says **hello** to Raju.

help: when you do something for someone

Nisha is **helping** mummy with the dishes.

hen: a bird that lays eggs

hide: to move or keep away from sight
The dog **hides** under the table.

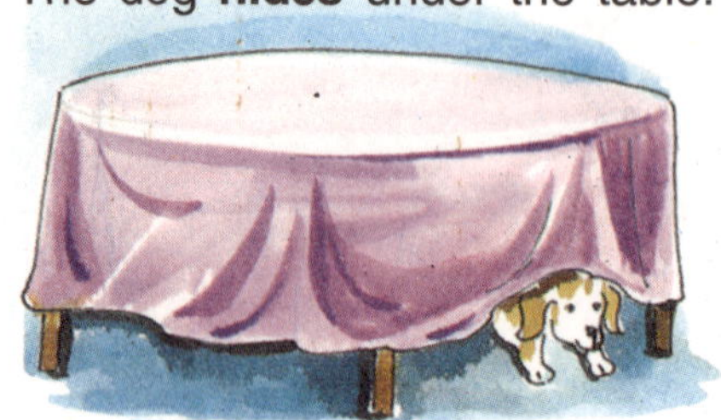

high: is far up

The building is **high**.

The boy jumps **high**.

hill: raised part of a land

Big **hills** are mountains.

hole; a hollow place

The sock has a **hole**.

holiday: a day of rest
A Sunday is a **holiday**.

home: is where both men and animals live.

There are many kinds of **homes**.

hop: when you jump on one leg

Hop, step and jump!

horn

Animals have **horns**.

Horn is a musical instrument.

Cars have **horns** too.

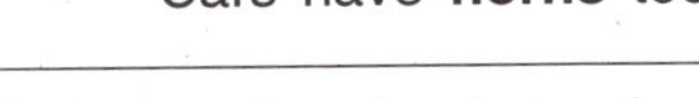

horse: a four-legged animal

A **horse** pulls a cart.

hospital: a place to recover from illness

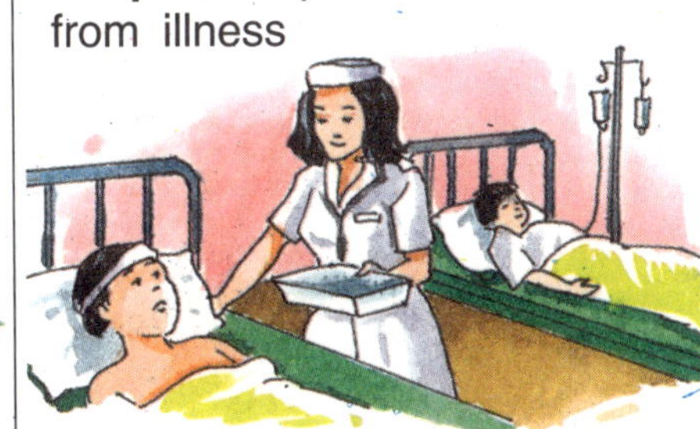

hot: when something is very warm

Soup is taken **hot**.

hotel: a home for travellers

Hotels have many rooms.

hour: is a measure of time

There are sixty minutes in an **hour**.

house: is where we live.

how: the way in which you do something or feel

Hirak is learning **how** to play the piano.

The doctor sees **how** the child feels.

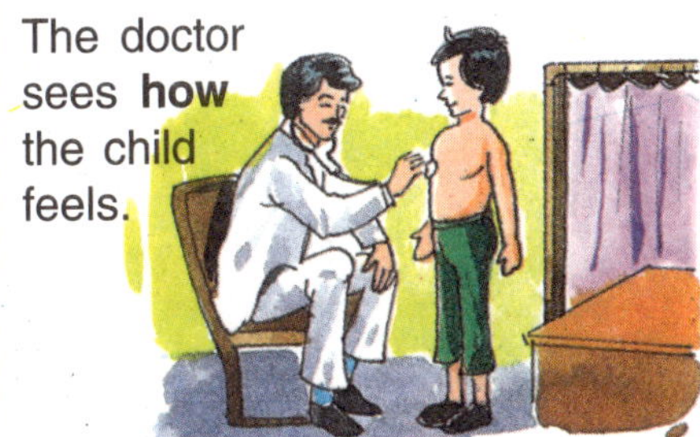

hungry: when you want to eat food

This dog is **hungry**.

hurry: to do something quickly

Hari is **hurrying** home.

hurt: to have an injury

Hari has **hurt** his arm.

i I

ice: frozen water

Ice keeps food cold in a fridge.

ice-cream: is cold and sweet to eat.

Rahul is enjoying an **ice-cream**.

icicle: formed when water freezes.

Icicles can hang from trees.

idea: an interesting thought or plan

Hari tells Rahul he has an **idea**.

ill: being unwell.

Anil is **ill**.

ink: is the liquid used in pens

There is blue **ink** in this bottle.

insect: a small creature with six legs

All these are **insects**.

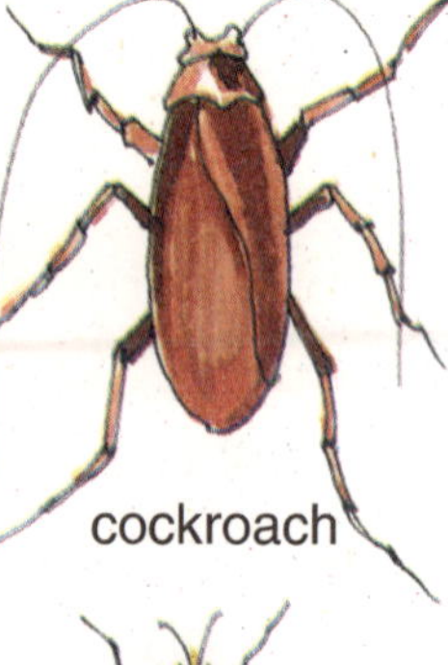

inside: means within

There is a mouse **inside** the box.

invite: to ask people over

Radha **invites** Anil to her birthday party.

iron: a hard metal

An **iron** presses clothes.

island: is the land surrounded by water

Sri Lanka is an **island**.

j J

jacket: what you wear on top of your shirt

Seema is wearing a **jacket**.

job: work you get paid for

Teaching is a **job**.

Driving is a **job** too.

jug: something which holds liquid

This **jug** holds orange juice.

jam: made with fruits and sugar

You eat **jam** with bread.

joke: something which makes people laugh

Joy prepares to play a **joke** on his daddy.

jump: to leap

Rina **jumps** over the skipping rope.

jeans: a type of trousers

Jeet is relaxing in his blue **jeans**.

journey: when people move from one place to another

We make **journeys** on bus, train and aeroplane.

jungle: a dense forest

Many wild animals and birds live in a **jungle**.

jelly: a sweet clear custard

Jellyfish is found in the sea.

judge: one who decides about something

Ms Sen is **judging** which onions are the best.

just: when it is exact

The clock shows it is **just** 2 o'clock.

k K

keep: to put something in its place

Karan **keeps** his bike in the shed.

kiss: to touch the skin with your lips

Anita **kisses** her doll.

knee: the point where the leg bends

key: something used to open locks with

kitchen: a room where food is cooked

knife: used for cutting

Both the **knives** are sharp.

kick: to hit

Rahul **kicks** the ball.

kite: a square or rectangular piece of paper that is made to fly

Ramu is flying a **kite**.

knock: to tap at the door

Karan is **knocking** at the door.

kind

The boy is **kind** to his rabbit.

What **kind** of rabbit is it?

kitten: a young cat

The **kitten** holds the kite's string.

knot: something that is tied

The parcel is tied with **knots**.

l L

ladder: a set of steps that can be moved

lazy: a person who does not like to work.

Who is **lazy** in this picture?

left: the other side of right

Lila holds a ball in her **left** hand.

Lalit holds up his **left** foot.

lamb: baby sheep

lead: whoever is in the front

One who **leads** is a leader.

letter: units of the alphabet

We write **letters** to keep in touch.

Letters are posted in a **letter** box.

large: big in size

This is a **large** leaf.

leaf: a part of a plant

Leaves are mostly green.

library: a place where you can borrow books from

Children are reading books in the **library**.

late: not being on time

Lalit is **late** for school.

leave: when you keep something in its place

leave: when you go away

lid: the cover of a pan

Eyelids cover the eyes.

lie: to rest in bed

Ramesh **lies** on the bed.

lie: to speak untruth

lift: to pick up

The man **lifts** a box of fruits.

A **lift** carries you to different floors of a building.

light: not heavy, like a feather or hanky

There is **sunlight** during the day.

like: to be fond of

Do you **like** to play with this ball?

line: a row

The children are standing in a **line**.

lip A mouth has two **lips**.

You use your **lips** to speak.

listen: to hear

Rahul **listens** to music.

loaf: a whole bread

This **loaf** is very delicious.

lock: to shut

You open **locks** with a key.

look: to see

Lila **looks** into the mirror.

Rahul **looks** at the bird.

loud: a noise that is heard

The children are making a **loud** noise with musical instruments.

low: short

The bush is **lower** than the tree.

lunch: the meal eaten in the afternoon

These three children are having their **lunch**.

m M

machine: an apparatus that helps us in our work

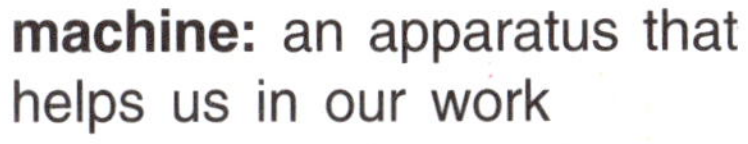

Computer, sewing machine, engine, vacuum cleaner, oven are all **machines**.

computer

map: it gives us directions

Maps also show countries.

march: to walk briskly in matching steps

magic: tricks to fool you
The **magician** has pulled a dove from the hat.

man
A young boy grows up to become a **man**.

make: to do something with one's hands

Mukesh is **making** a house.

Ali is **making** a figure.

many: more than one

There are **many** balls inside the box.

mark: the point that sets the line.

On your **mark** – get, set, go!

meet: to come together
Ladies **meet** in the market.

market: a place where things are bought and sold

mirror: the glass in which we see ourselves.

Rina is looking at the **mirror**.

mat: a small rug

The cat is sitting on a **mat**.

melt: when snow becomes water

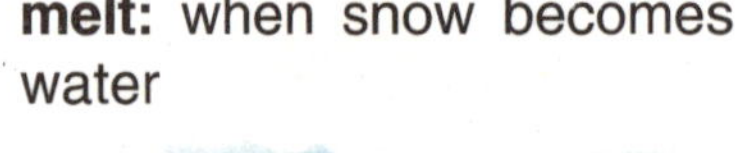

The snow of the mountain is **melting**.

miss

miss: to fail to hit or reach

Rahul **misses** the bull's eye.

match: when two things are similar

Radha's clothes **match**.

A **match** is used to light a fire.

A game can be a **match**.

middle: is the centre of something

Rahul is standing in the **middle** of his friends.

Manoj **misses** his school bus.

milk: a liquid we drink

Cows give us **milk**.

mistake: an error

Has Mina put salt in her milk by **mistake**?

measure: to find the size of something

Mrs Rai **measures** milk.
Mr Rai **measures** cloth.

minute: a unit of time

Sixty **minutes** make an hour.

mix: when you put things together

Mrs Rai is **mixing** the flour for a cake.

money: a unit with what you buy things

Coins and notes are **money**.

monkey: an animal that lives on trees

Have you seen a **monkey** at the zoo?

month
30 days make a **month**
Twelve **months** make what?

January	February	March
April	May	June
July	August	September
October	November	December

moon: a big natural body that shines at night

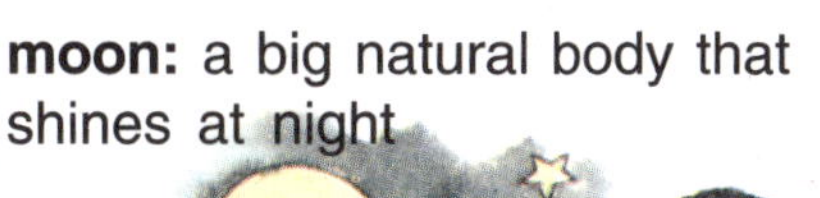

A **moon** changes its shape.

more: not less

Rima wants **more** cake.

morning: the first part of day

We brush our teeth in the **morning**.

mountain: a big hill

mouse: a small furry animal

more than one **mouse** is known as **mice**.

mouth

We use our **mouth** to talk and eat with.

move: to go from one place to another

The dog **moves** the bone to another hole.

much: a large amount or quantity of something

"How much do the mangoes cost?" Mihir asks the mango-seller.

music: the melody we make with instruments

Name these musical **instruments**.

nail: the sharp point in our hands and feet

The **nails** of animals are known as claws.

near: to be close

The dog sits **near** his owner.

neighbour: someone who stays next door

nearly: almost there

Nitin **nearly** won the race.

neither: not one or the other

Nisha wants **neither** of the sweets.

name: what we are called by

What is your **name**?

neck: the part that connects the head with the body

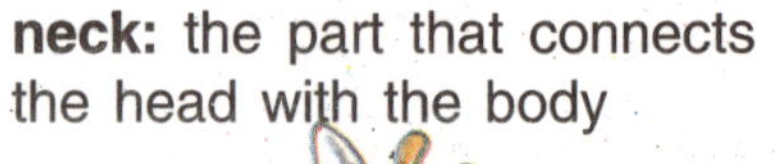

Nisha's **neck** is short.

The giraffe's **neck** is long.

nest: a bird's home

Birds build their own **nests** with twigs.

narrow: the space that is not wide

The fence has a **narrow** gap.

need: to want something

Rahul is thirsty, he **needs** water.

never: not ever

Never put anything sharp on a switchboard.

new: not old

The green car is not **new**.

news: it tells us what is happening around us

Letters too bring in **news**.

A **newspaper** prints news.

News is read on television.

next: what comes after

The letter box is **next** to the post office building.

Doctor calls the **next** patient.

night: comes after daytime

The stars and moon shine at **night**.

nine: a number between eight and ten

How many flowers can you see? **Nine**!

nobody: when there is no one.

Nobody is in the classroom.

noise: a loud sound

The dog's bark is **noisy**.

none: not a single one

None of the children are wearing uniform.

nose We breathe and smell with our **nose**.

number
A **number** tells us how many.

1	2	3	4
5	6	7	8
9	10	11	12
13	14	15	16
17	18	19	20

Do you know the **numbers** from 1 to 20?

nurse: one who looks after to the sick people

A **nurse** wears a uniform.

nut: is the seed of plants

Nuts are of various kinds: peanuts, walnuts.

o O

oak: a kind of tree
Acorn is the fruit of the **oak** tree.

office

Men and women work in an **office**.

once: once means at one time.

Once upon a time, kings ruled.

ocean: a very large sea

Big ships sail on **oceans**.

oil: liquid used to run cars or cook food

one: the single number

Harsh has **one** grey glove and **one** white glove.

odd: when something is different

Spot the **odd** sock.

We use **oil** to cook our food.

only: one of its kind

Only one sweet is red.

off: not on

Harsh turns **off** the radio.

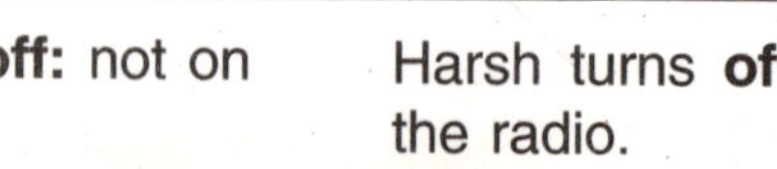

The ball rolls **off** the table.

old: not new

This railway engine is **old**.

open: when it is not closed

The window and door are **open**.

orange: a kind of fruit

The colour of the fruit is **orange** too.

orchard: where many trees grow

Can you name the fruits growing in this **orchard**?

order: a command

An officer shouts an **order** to the soldiers.

Mummy **orders** Nisha to study.

organ: a musical instrument

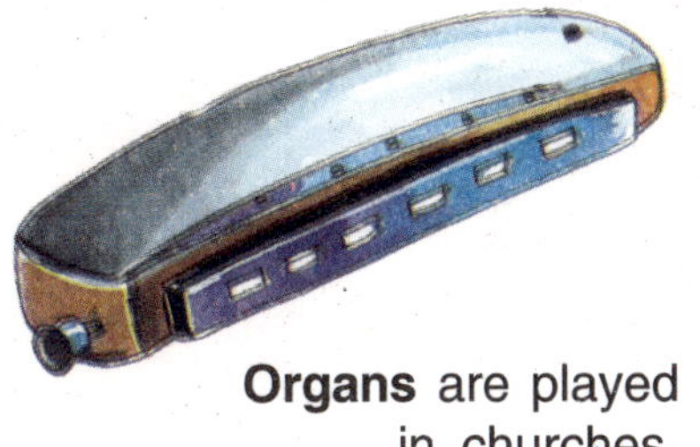

Organs are played in churches.

other: when it is not the one

Radha tries the **other** hats.

out: not within

The children are looking **out** of the window.

outdoors: outside the house

Nisha is **outdoors**.

outside: not inside

The children are playing **outside** their house.

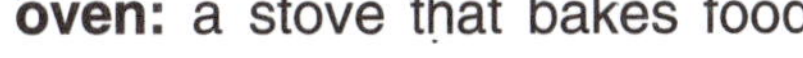

oven: a stove that bakes food

Buns are in this **oven**.

over: above. When something ends

Is the programme on TV **over**?

The girl holds an umbrella **over** her head.

Also means more – There are **over** 20 nails.

overalls: worn over your clothes

Painters wear **overalls**.

owl: a bird which is seen at night

An **owl** has round eyes.

own: when it belongs to someone

This is Nisha's **own** parrot.

p P

page
Books and newspapers have **pages**

This book has many **pages**.

pain: an ache or a hurt

Paul has a **pain** in his knee.

A **palm** is also a kind of tree.

parent: a **parent** is a father or mother

Amit is standing with his **parents**.

park: an open space with grass and trees

You play in a **park**.

paint: to colour pictures

Daddy **paints** the door.
Amit **paints** the picture.

paper

We write and draw on **paper**.

party: when friends get together for fun

This is a birthday **party**.

palm: the inside of your hand

pavement: the path besides the road

We walk on the **pavements**.

pay: when you give money for something

Nita **pays** for Tina's ticket.

A **pen** writes with ink.

We also write with **pencils**.

people

Men, women and children are all **people**.

Human beings are all **people**.

pet: an animal we take care of at home

All these are **pets**.

picnic: an outdoor party

Picnics are fun.

picture: a drawing

Mr. Puri is drawing a **picture**.

piece: the part that is cut from a whole thing

Pradeep has cut the cake into **pieces**.

pile: to make a heap

Priya sweeps the leaves into a **pile**.

pin: to fasten things

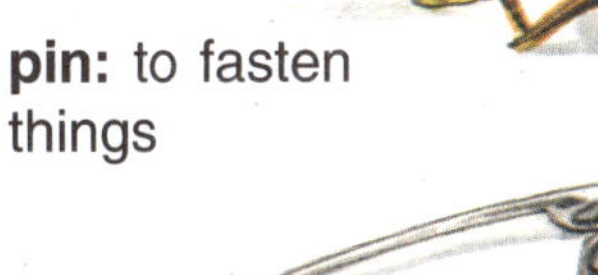

These are different types of **pins**.

plant

Trees, grass, bushes are all **plants**.

Daddy is **planting** some bulbs. He is putting them in the ground.

plate: a big saucer

Food is eaten from a **plate**.

play: a show in which people act

You **play** games like hockey, cricket.

You **play** the guitar.

playground: a place where you play

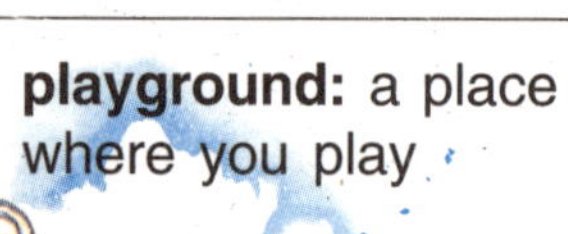

A **playground** has a slide, a swing and a sea-saw.

pocket

Sonia has a toy clown in the **pocket** of her dress.

pond: a pool of water

Ducks swim in a **pond**.

pony: a small horse

post: to send a letter you have to **post** it

A **postman** delivers letters.

prize: a reward or trophy for doing something well

Rahul's picture has won him a **prize**.

pull: to stretch out

The children are **pulling** the two ends of a rope.

puppet: a doll that is moved on a string

Puppets often tell a story.

push: to apply force to move something

The man is **pushing** a wheelbarrow.

put: to place something on something else

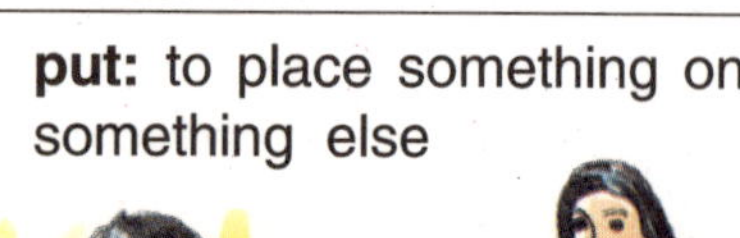

Rahul **puts** on his shirt.

puzzle: a riddle

Paul is doing a jigsaw **puzzle**.

q Q

quack: the call of ducks

The duck is **quacking**.

question: to ask something

The teacher **questions** the students.

quiet: not to make a noise

"**Quiet**, the baby sleeps," says mummy.

quantity: a measure of things

Daddy has ordered a large **quantity** of bricks.

queue: to stand orderly in a row

The children **queue** at a bus stop.

quilt: a warm blanket.

We use **quilts** in winter.

quarrel: to fight over something

The children are **quarreling** over a bag.

quite: when we compare two things

Nisha is not **quite** as tall as Rahul.

quarter: is one of four equal parts

The apple has been cut into **quarters**.

quick: fast

Nisha runs **quickly**.

quiz: a test to measure one's knowledge

People doing a **quiz** have to answer questions.

r R

race: it decides who can run faster

Arun and Raj are having a **race**.

rain: drops of water as they fall from clouds

rainbow

We see a **rainbow** when the sun shines through rain.

raw: when food is not cooked

Which foods do we eat **raw**?

reach: to seek something

Rahul cannot **reach** the jam jar.

real: not false

Which is the **real** rabbit?

red: a colour
Roses are mostly **red**.

This is a **red** apple.

remember: when you think back

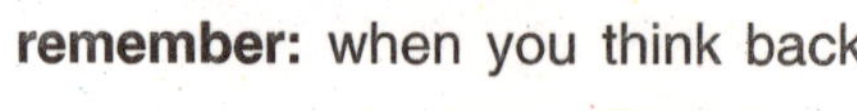

The opposite of **remember** is forget.

rest: it separates one thing from another

One ball is green, the **rest** are blue.

rest: to relax.

Romit **rests** as he is tired.

riddle: a puzzle

Harsh is puzzled over a **riddle**.

ride: to move on something

We **ride** on a bicycle or on a horse.

right: the other side of left

Romit shows his **right** hand.

not wrong – Ram has got all his sums **right**.

ring: an ornament for the finger

A circus has a **ring** in the centre.

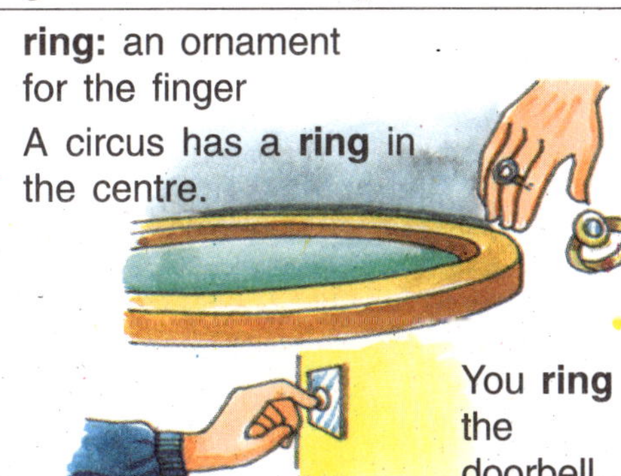

You **ring** the doorbell.

river: a large stream of water

road: cars and buses travel on **roads**

We cross the **road** at a crossing.

rock: a hard stone.

A rocking chair **rocks** back and forth.

roll: a long piece of bread.

You fold a carpet by **rolling** it.

The marbles **roll** across the floor.

Ronit also **rolls** on the floor.

roof: the top covering of a house

A crow sits on a **roof**.

room: you live inside a **room**

A house has many **rooms**.

rough: not smooth

The sea is **rough**.

The egg is not **rough**, it is smooth.

round: the shape of a circle

All objects in this picture are **round**.

row: arranged in a straight line

The flowers are planted in a **row**.

You **row** a boat with oars.

run: to move quickly

The boy and the dog are **running**.

s S

sack: a large bag to store things

The children are in a **sack** race.

scare: frighten

Sohail is trying to **scare** Shiela. She is not **scared**.

sea: a vast body of salty water

Have you been to a **seaside**?

same: when two things are alike

Shiela has the **same** books.

sand: tiny pieces of rock

Sand is found on beaches and deserts

school: the place where you study

Which **school** do you study in?

season

A year is divided into four **seasons**: summer, spring, autumn and winter.

save: to **save** is to keep something

Nishi **saves** her money. She is **saving** to buy a doll.

scissors

We cut hair and paper with a pair of **scissors**.

seat: something you sit on

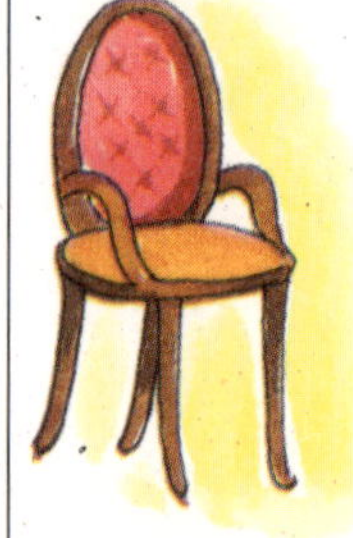

A chair is a **seat**.

A stool is a **seat** too.

seed

Plants grow from **seeds**.

Some **seeds** are fruits.

sell: to give something for money

This shop **sells** fruits.

sense: to feel

Our **senses** help us to taste, smell and feel.

seven: a number between six and eight

These are **seven** swans.

shape

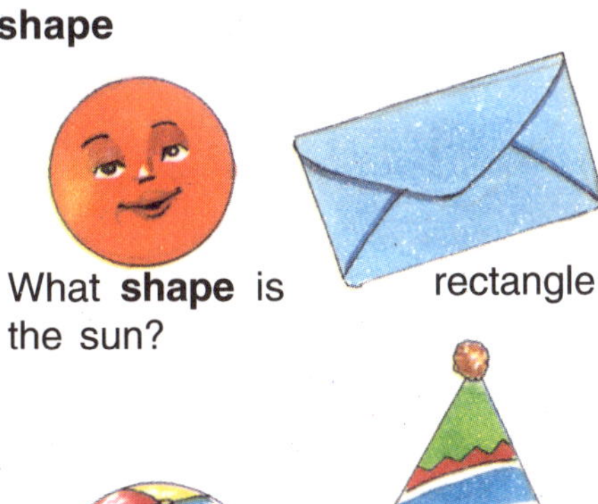

What **shape** is the sun?

rectangle

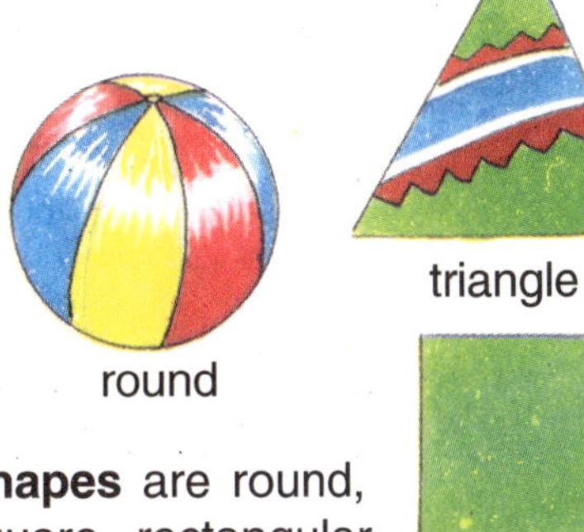

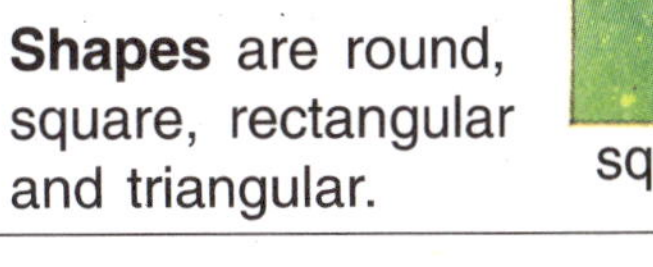

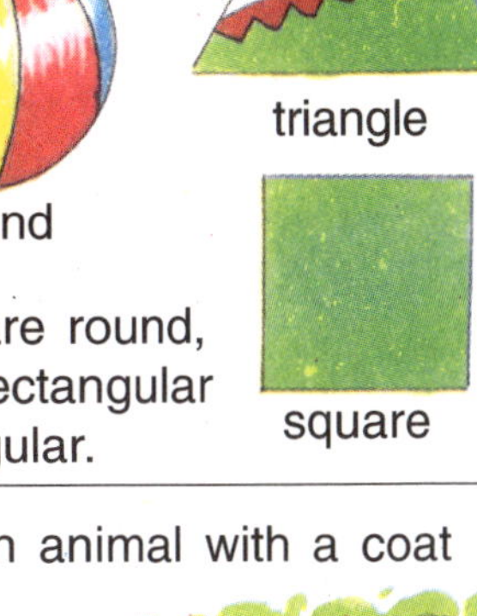

triangle

round

square

Shapes are round, square, rectangular and triangular.

sheep: an animal with a coat of wool

We make warm clothes from **sheep** wool.

shell: an outer covering

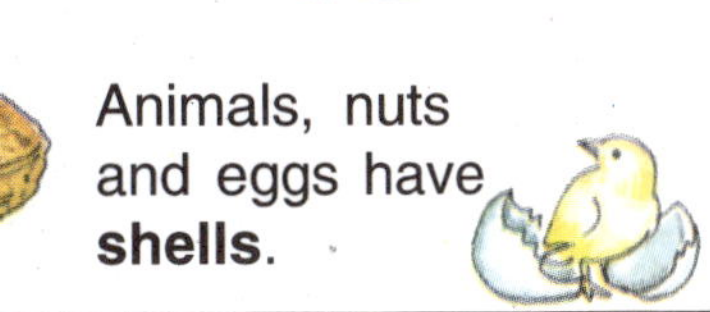

Animals, nuts and eggs have **shells**.

ship: a very big boat

Ships sail on seas.

shoes: footwear to cover our feet

Horses wear **shoes** too.

shop: a building where many things are sold to public

A market has many **shops**.

shut: when something is closed

The window and the door are **shut**.

sing: when we make a sweet sound with our voice

Birds too **sing**.

six: a number between five and seven

These are **six** spades.

size: tells us how big or small a thing is

Shoes have different **sizes**.

Packages have different **sizes**.

skates

We wear **skates** to move on the floor.

skin: the covering of our body

Fruits have **skin** too.

sky: the sky is the space above the earth

What colour is the **sky** today?

sleep: when we rest our body and mind

Amit is **sleeping**.

smile

We express our happiness with a **smile**.

smoke: fumes that come from fire

Smoke from cigarettes is harmful.

smooth: when a surface is without any bumps

This piece of cloth feels **smooth**.

snake: a long animal without legs

A **snake** crawls on the ground.

snow: frozen water which turns white

Children make a **snowman** out of **snow**.

soap: something that helps us keep clean

We bathe with **soap** and wash our hands with **soap**.

soft: not hard.
Not loud.
Suresh's head is on a **soft** pillow.

Mummy speaks in a **soft** voice.

sound: something heard by our ears

We hear different **sounds**.

speak: to talk

A teacher is **speaking** to her students.

stairs: steps that connect floors

stick: a straight piece of wood

An old man uses a **stick** to walk.

street: is a small road in a town or city

People are walking on the **street**.

stamp

Before you post a letter, you fix a **stamp** on the envelope.

Suresh **stamps** his feet in anger.

stop: to halt

Buses **stop** at bus stops and traffic lights.

strong: to have strength

This **strong** man can lift weights.

start: to begin

The runners wait at the **start**.

storm In a **storm**, the wind blows hard.

In a **storm**, you hear thunder and see lightning.

sun: a ball of fire

Sun gives us light and warmth.

star: distant bodies of light that twinkle in the sky

Shiela draws a **star**.

story: a tale that is told or read

The grandmother tells us a **story**.

sweep: to clean a place of dirt

The sweeper **sweeps** up the litter.

stay: to wait

The boy tells the dog to **stay** in one place.

swim: to float and move around in water without sinking

Sohan is **swimming** in the river.

t T

Table
Tables have a flat top on which we work or eat

A **table** has legs too.

taste: to feel with your tongue

Gulab jamuns are sweet in **taste**.

television

A **television** beams pictures and sound.

tail: animals have **tails**

This monkey has a long **tail**.

taxi: a hired car

Taxis are mostly yellow and black in colour

ten: a number between nine and eleven

These are **ten** tops.

tall: very high

Tall
taller
tallest

Rohan is **tall**.

Sohan is **taller**.

Mohan is **tallest**.

tea: a hot drink made with tea leaves

Mohan is **drinking** tea.

tent: used outdoors to sit and sleep in

Sohan is sitting inside the **tent**.

telephone

A **telephone** helps us to speak to people far away.

thick: not thin

The book is **thick**.
Tony wears a **thick** sweater.

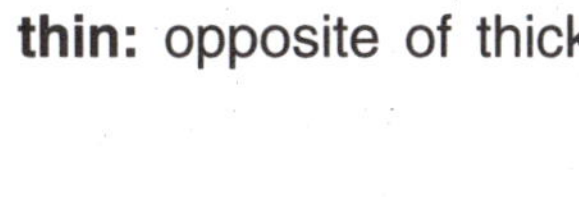

thin: opposite of thick

This paper is **thin**.

The man is **thin**.

thirsty: is when your throat gets dry

Tarun drinks water as he is **thirsty**.

three: a number between two and four

These are **three** lion heads.

thumb

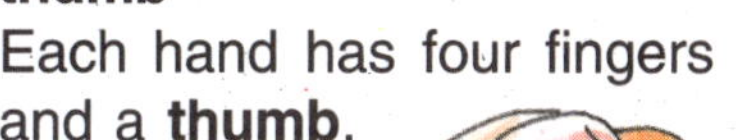

Each hand has four fingers and a **thumb**.

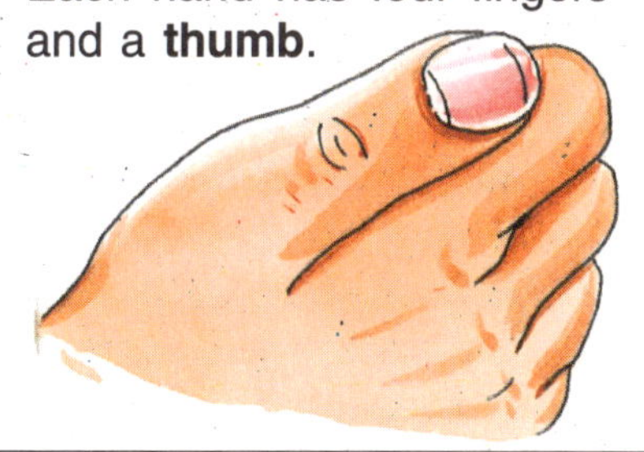

thunder: the loud noise we hear after lightning

In storms, we often hear **thunder** and see lightning.

ticket: a piece of paper needed for travel

To watch a film, you need a **ticket** too.

tie: worn around the neck

Rima is **tying** a gift.

Vijay is wearing a tie.

time: tells us what part of the day it is.

Watches and clocks tell us the **time**.

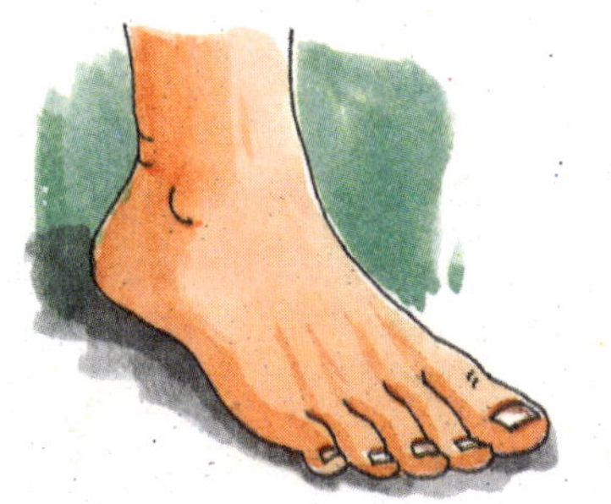

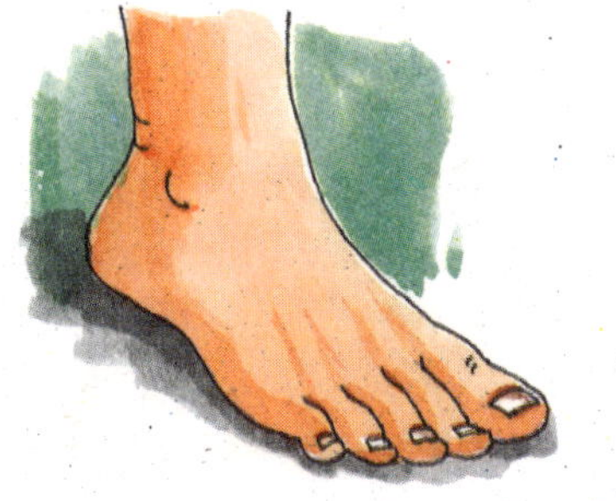

toes: the five fingers in our feet

together: to be with someone

The boys are playing **together**.

The cats are sitting **together**.

tongue: the organ we taste with

Anil tastes the ice-cream with his **tongue**.

The frog's **tongue** is big.

tool: an object that helps us in our work

Hammer, hoe and saw are **tools**.

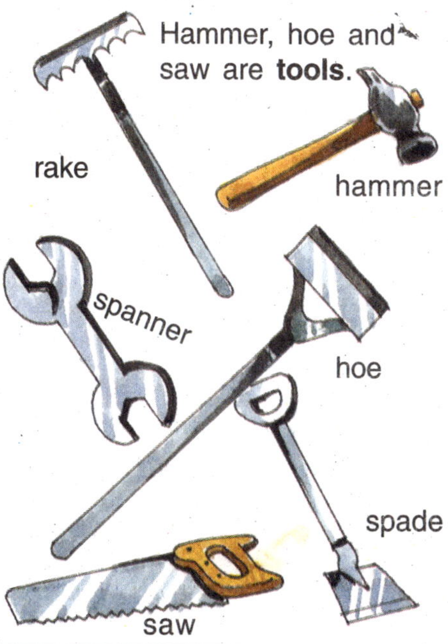

tooth: More than one tooth is **teeth**.

Teeth help us eat and talk.

We brush our **teeth** with a toothbrush.

Tarun has lost a **tooth**.

top: to be above

The cat from the **top** watches a spinning **top**.

touch: means feel

The girls **touch** hands.

town: a small city

A **town** is bigger than a village.

toy: the things children play with

Name these **toys**.

train

We travel by **trains**.

to teach – Rahul **trains** his dog.

tree: a very big plant

There are many kinds of **trees**.

true: when something really happens

"Is it **true** you got wet?" Tina asks Tarun.

twelve: a number between eleven and thirteen; also known as a dozen

There are **twelve** shirts.

twins: two children born on the same day to same parents

Mohan and Rohan are **twins**.

two: a number between one and three

There are **two** tomatoes and **two** turtles.

typewriter: a writing machine

A typist is typing a letter on a **typewriter**.

tyre

Cars and buses move on **tyres**.

This car has a flat **tyre**.

u U

umbrella: a head cover that keeps off rain

Umbrellas can be folded.

underwear: what we wear inside our clothes

upstairs: the upper part of the house

Mummy is walking **upstairs**.

The dog is already **upstairs**.

under: when something is below

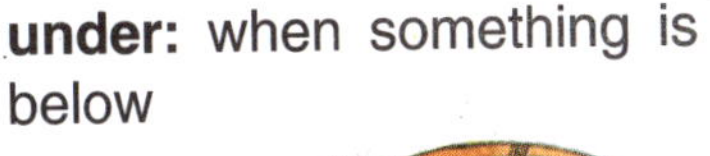

The cat is **under** the chair.

uniform: a same set of clothes for all

The children wear school **uniforms**.

use: to do something with

Uma is **using** a camera.

A string has many **uses**.

underground: the space below the ground

Many things are there **underground**.

up: means high above

A bird flies **up** in the sky.

understand: to know something well

Mummy helps Umesh **understand** his lessons.

upside down: turned the wrong way

The boy is hanging **upside** down.

useful: things which help

Paints are **useful** in colouring pictures and houses.

v V

valley: the land between two hills

A river flows through the **valley**.

value: means the worth

The **value** of this bicycle is Rs.1,500.

van

A **van** transports people and things.

vase: a holder for flowers

This is a very beautiful **vase**.

vegetable: food that grows on plants

potato

gourd

pea

carrot

brinjal

cauliflower

cabbage

bean

tomato

onion

village: a very small town

This **village** is near the city.

violin: a musical instrument with four strings. It is played with a bow.

visit: to go and meet

Did you **visit** your grandparents?

voice

We use our **voice** to speak and sing with.

volcano: a crater on a mountain top

A **volcano** gives out lava.

w W

wait: to stay in a place
Mummy asks Raj to **wait** for her.

watch: an apparatus that shows us the time

to view – Rahul **watches** TV.

week

A **week** has seven days.

walk: to go by foot

Daddy is **walking** with his dog.
Nitin **walks** with him.

water
We drink **water** when thirsty

Water is found in ponds.
Rain is **water** too.

Sunday
Monday
Tuesday
Wednesday
Thursday
Friday
Saturday

wall: a **wall** divides an area of land

These are brick **walls**.

wash: to clean with water

We **wash** hands.

The dhobi **washes** clothes.

weather: tells us what season it is

windy

cold

hot

rainy

weigh: a measure to see how heavy a thing is

The man **weighs** sweets.

Rahul **weighs** himself.

wet: covered with water

Mummy hangs out the **wet** clothes.

whale: world's biggest animal

Whales are found in oceans.

wheels

Wheels are round and make things move.

whisper: to talk very softly

Ritika **whispers** into Rahul's ears.

white: a colour

Cow is **white**.

Clouds are **white** too.

whole: the complete thing

Rahul is eating a **whole** apple.

win: to leave others behind.

Nitin **wins** the race.

window

Windows let in the air and sunlight.

wings

Birds fly with the help of **wings**.

woman: a grown-up girl

Mummy is a **woman**.

work: when we do something

Mummy **works** as a housewife.

Farmer, postman and teacher – all **work**.

world: the place we all live in.

The **world** is made up of many countries.

write: when we put words on paper

wrong: not right

"Your sum is **wrong**," the teacher tells Rahul.

x X

y Y

Xmas

Xmas is another way of saying Christmas.

yacht: a small boat with big sails

yell: to shout loudly

yawn: to open our mouth wide

We **yawn** when tired.

yellow: a colour

The bird is yellow

A banana is **yellow** too.

The sunflower is **yellow**.

x-ray

An **x-ray** takes pictures of the inside of our bodies.

year: measures time

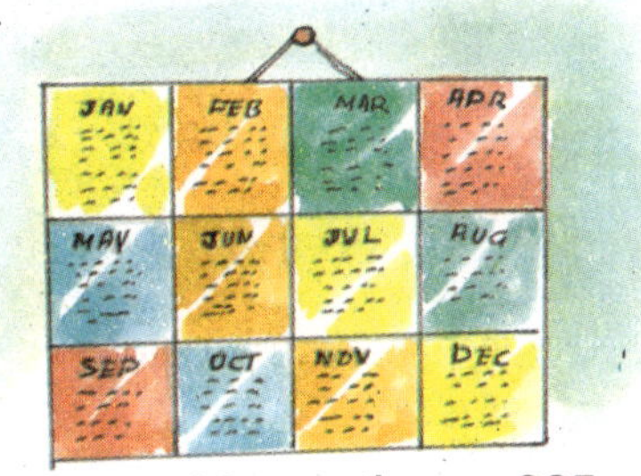

There are 12 months or 365 days in a **year**.

yes

When you agree, you say **yes**. "**Yes**, I'll come to your party," Rahul says to Ajay.

xylophone

A **xylophone** produces music.

You play a **xylophone** with wooden sticks.

yesterday: the day before today is **yesterday**

If today is Tuesday, **yesterday** was Monday.

y Y

yolk: the yellow part of the egg

young: not old

A kitten is a **young** cat.
A pup is a **young** dog.

your: what belongs to you

Touch **your** head.
Clap **your** hands.

yo-yo: a toy that bounces on a string

z Z

zebra: a horse-like animal with black and white stripes

Have you seen a **zebra** at the zoo?

zero: nothing; the starting point

zigzag: when a path is not straight

Zigzag is a side-to-side movement.

zip: fastens two things

Anil **zips** his jacket as it is cold.

zoo: where you can see animals and birds

Have you seen these animals at the **zoo**?

tiger penguin

elephant seal

lion deer

bear